Sunday with the Family Circus®

By
Bil Keane

JUDSON PRESS®   •   VALLEY FORGE

SUNDAYS ARE HAPPY DAYS IN A HOME where there is love—and so are Mondays through Saturdays. The Sunday feeling I try to portray in my cartoons is one of love and respect for another, whether it is Mommy's and Daddy's for the children, the children's for one another and their parents, or the entire family's love for God.

Those little irritating and frustrating moments we all experience are really funny—in retrospect. That "crisis" today could well be one of your happiest memories. As you read through this collection of cartoons, you are sure to come across situations that have taken place in your home. If you didn't laugh at them when they happened, here is a second chance.

No sound on earth is more heavenly than the cheerful chirping of youngsters as they experience the surprising world unfolding around them day after day. Parents who can smile with understanding, pleasure, and tolerance through the chirping will enjoy to the fullest each phase of family life year after year.

Treasure the years your children are young—they are all too fleeting. But welcome also the constant change and growth as the little ones mature and the family becomes even more interesting and exciting.

True humor is insight. Insight is warmth. Warmth is love.

Much love from The Family Circus, gentle reader—we are happy to have you spend this Sunday with us.

Bil
Keane

"He's half awake—you open the other eye."

"Today's SUNDAY, Daddy! The church bells woked me up!"

"We'll be late for church all because you didn't sound off on time!"

"I don't think I can sing with the choir—I have a headache in my throat."

"Daddy's shaving!"

"When we get our own cereal on Sundays it saves you a lot of work, right, Mommy?"

"They're waffles, dear—not 'awfuls.' "

"How many things shall I take to church to keep me quiet?"

"When I get washed do I have to do my hands, too?"

"Which one goes on which foot?"

"I tied my own shoe laces!"

"Mommy, the sleeves of my pants are getting too short."

"How do you know I'm going to pinch your neck?
I haven't even started to BUTTON it yet!"

"There's no hole for this button!"

"No dear, I'm not locking him up—this is a bunting."

"I'll be ready as soon as I polish my other shoe."

SUNDAY WITH THE FAMILY CIRCUS

"All systems are go, but one."

"We're just one shoe away from leaving."

"Daddy, why does your right foot stamp the floor whenever we come to a corner?"

"Do you still have the dime Daddy gave you last Sunday?"

SUNDAY WITH THE FAMILY CIRCUS

"HERE, BOY!"

"Jeffy's tummy is talking in church."

SUNDAY WITH THE FAMILY CIRCUS

"Oooh, Mommy! He said a BAD word!"

"Pass it on."

"Why are your eyes closed, Daddy?"

SUNDAY WITH THE FAMILY CIRCUS

"Why did he say 'God bless you'? Nobody sneezed."

"I forgot to say one for Barfy!"

"Barfy is so glad to see us home from church he's doing the twist!"

"I'm a big help now, Mommy—I can take my own coat off!"

"Today's Billy's first day at Sunday School and he'll be bouncing in any minute bursting to tell everything that happened."

"MOMMY! I'm home from Sunday School!"

"When the class sings hymns, Miss Madelaine
says I'm to be a 'listener'!"

"And when it was my turn to tell the Sunday School class about my home, I just said we live over a garage."

"Time to set the table."

"Shall I put out the cloth napkins, or aren't Grandma and Grandad 'company'?"

"Why can't I have my piece of turkey with a handle on it like Dolly and Billy?"

"Grandma, if you're REALLY Daddy's mother, why don't you ever yell at him or spank him?"

"Hello, there! Run and tell Mommy the president of the Church Ladies' Aid would like to see her."

"I'll be with you in a minute—won't you sit down?"

"Which do you want to hear me sing—a church hymn or a TV commercial?"

"Well, if all the kids are napping, can your father come out and play?"

"You better not step on my shoes—Daddy just shined them."

"My guardian angel pushed me!"

"Get him quick—before he prays his way out of this!"

"Can't you pretend you're driving us to church without making that awful noise?"

"I think we've landed in Uncle Wiggily's cabbage patch and have to go back to 'START.' "

"Billy washed my face with snow and that's a SIN, isn't it, Mommy?"

"I think it's one of ours—at least the sniffle is the same as the one we kept hearing in church this morning."

"Grownups can do anything—Why does Daddy LIKE Sunday naps?"

"Hey, that's pretty good, Daddy! What's it spell?"

"CR-R-UNCH!"

"Guess who set the table."

"Do you want to try yours on your lap for a while, Daddy, or shall I put it right on the floor?"

"This tastes so good it seems like we're eating out!"

"Why did you turn the radio up so loud, Daddy?"

SUNDAY WITH THE FAMILY CIRCUS

"Strange—only vegetables and meat on the floor.
Not a scrap of pie."

"But, Mommy, I need the cans for a Sunday School project."

"PJ! Look, PJ! That's a good baby— THERE! Got him smiling!"

"Now, you be good children for Grandma while I'm at church."

"NOBODY'S coming! It's Sunday and I just want
all these things picked up!"

"Here's the church and there's the steeple . . ."

"That organ music makes me happy—it sounds like church!"

"I want to talk to somebody in Heaven."

"Come on, PJ, you can learn it—OUR FATHER WHO ART IN HEAVEN, HAROLD BE THY NAME..."

"Can't hear you, Mommy—Can you read it noisier?"

"THE END—and that finishes our Bible stories for tonight."

"I'm sure it's just some kind of bug he's picked up at Sunday School."

SUNDAY WITH THE FAMILY CIRCUS

"If everybody'll be quiet you'll be able to hear me
saying my prayers!"

"That's about all for tonight—I'll call again in the morning."

"Can I throw in a commercial about a new bike?"

"Can you start me out with my prayers again? I forgot to 'God Bless' the people next door."

"I thought it was my guardian angel flying around,
'til it bit me."

"Can I use this for my Easter basket?"

"I don't feel well."

"Shall I put on my new Easter pants again today?"

"Better put a card with it so Mommy will know who it's from."

"I need a sweet potato and a jar for Sunday School, but don't look at them. We're making something for Mother's Day."

"Which of the things you got for Father's Day did you like best, Daddy?"

"Are you sure God will know it's me?"

"Mary and Joseph should have come to OUR house! We have room—and we even have a crib!"

"Better be good—Santa Claus is watching us."

"Very nice! But how did the cowboy and the
dinosaur get there?"

"Then Joseph got Mary off the donkey and they went into the stable and found Baby Jesus in the hay."

"We're wrapping PJ in swaddling clothes."

"Happy Birthday to You . . ."